Who Was
Bruce Lee?

Who Was Bruce Lee?

By Jim Gigliotti

Illustrated by John Hinderliter

Grosset & Dunlap
An Imprint of Penguin Group (USA) LLC

GROSSET & DUNLAP
Published by the Penguin Group
Penguin Group (USA) LLC, 375 Hudson Street, New York, New York 10014, USA

USA | Canada | UK | Ireland | Australia | New Zealand | India | South Africa | China

penguin.com
A Penguin Random House Company

Text copyright © 2014 by Jim Gigliotti. Illustrations copyright © 2014 by Penguin Group (USA) LLC. Cover illustration copyright © 2014 by Nancy Harrison. All rights reserved. Published by Grosset & Dunlap, a division of Penguin Young Readers Group, 345 Hudson Street, New York, New York 10014. GROSSET & DUNLAP is a trademark of Penguin Group (USA) LLC. Printed in the USA.

Library of Congress Cataloging-in-Publication Data is available.

ISBN 978-0-448-47949-1   10 9 8 7 6 5

Contents

Who Was
Bruce Lee?

The spectators at the International Karate Tournament of 1964 in Long Beach, California were amazed. They were watching a twenty-three-year-old young man named Bruce Lee give a demonstration in martial arts. The martial arts are ways of fitness, fighting, and self-defense. Many of them began hundreds of years ago in Asia, in places such as China, Japan, and Korea.

First, Bruce did some push-ups. But these weren't ordinary push-ups. Bruce did them with only one hand. Not only that, he did them using only *two fingers* of one hand. Push-ups are hard enough to do with two hands. They're almost impossible with two fingers. But Bruce had no trouble. Up, down, up, down—perfect form. What strength Bruce had!

Then Bruce showed what he called a "one-inch punch." His opponent stood directly in front of him. Bruce pulled his hand back just one inch. He

thrust it forward with such force that the other man fell backward into a chair. The other man couldn't stay standing, even though he knew what was coming. What power Bruce had!

Finally, Bruce stood with his opponent right in front of him. Bruce stood perfectly still. Suddenly, Bruce's hands flashed and were in the other man's face before he could react. Bruce didn't hit him or even touch him. He was just showing how quick he could be. What speed Bruce had!

News of Bruce's amazing performance that day reached a Hollywood producer. He thought Bruce might be the right actor for a new television series. The part needed someone who could be a superspy, like a Chinese James Bond. So the producer asked Bruce to come in for a screen test—a tryout for television or the movies.

Bruce was a natural in front of the camera. He had a lot of experience acting when he was growing up in Hong Kong. He also had

confidence, charm, and good looks. He did so well in his screen test that he got the part! He was no longer "just" a martial-arts star. He was going to be a TV star, too.

Bruce accomplished many other things during his lifetime. He was also a teacher and an author. Most of all, though, he became known around the world as an action-movie star. He used his martial-arts skills in the movies to fight the bad guys and save the day.

Then suddenly, Bruce was gone. Even before his most successful movie was shown in theaters, he died. He was only thirty-two years old.

That was in 1973. Bruce Lee is even more famous now than he was then. Other actors and actresses have portrayed martial artists in the movies. But no one ever did it with the strength, power, and speed that Bruce did.

Chapter 1
Birth and Childhood

From the very beginning, Bruce Lee was constantly in motion. When he was a little boy, he was a bundle of energy. He was always playing, running, or jumping. He bounced around his family's apartment so much that his parents and brothers and sisters nicknamed him "Mo Si Ting," which means "never sits still."

Bruce was born in Chinatown of San Francisco, California. His given name was Jun Fan. The Chinese custom is to put the "last name" first, so his full name was Lee Jun Fan.

Bruce was born on November 27, 1940, in what the Chinese calendar considers the year of the dragon. The Chinese calendar also considers the hour he was born as the hour of the dragon (between 6:00 a.m. and 8:00 a.m.). So Bruce was sometimes called "the Dragon" or, when he was young, "Little Dragon." The dragon is an important symbol in Chinese culture. It is a sacred creature that brings power and good luck.

One of the nurses at the hospital in San Francisco gave Lee Jun Fan his Americanized name, Bruce.

Bruce's dad was named Lee Hoi Chuen. He was a well-known actor in a traveling Chinese opera that was in California at the time his son was born. He had also appeared in many movies in China. Bruce's mom was Grace Ho.

The Lee family included Bruce's older sisters, Phoebe and Agnes, his older brother, Peter, and his younger brother, Robert, who was born in 1948.

When he was just a few months old, Bruce and his family returned to Hong Kong, where his parents had been born. His dad's job meant Bruce was around the performing arts at a young age. He loved to go to work with his dad, and he soon appeared in movies himself. He had natural charisma on-screen and was in twenty films as a youngster.

Bruce didn't have quite the same enthusiasm for school, however. He was a smart kid, but he didn't try very hard—or he couldn't sit still long enough to try! When he was twelve years old he entered secondary school. All of his classes were in English. That was a new language for him. At home, his family spoke only Chinese. One day, Bruce's mother got frustrated with his performance in school. She asked him how he ever expected to make a living when he grew up.

"I'll become a famous film star one day," Bruce told her in Chinese.

Instead of studying, Bruce channeled his boundless energy into fighting. He became mixed up in the gang culture in Hong Kong. He led his own small gang called the Tigers.

"From boyhood to adolescence, I was a bit of a troublemaker and was greatly disapproved of by my elders," Bruce admitted later. "I was extremely mischievous and aggressive."

Bruce started getting into a lot of fights. One day, when he was about thirteen, he lost a fight and was beat up. He decided he had to learn to protect himself better. So he began to study the martial art called kung fu.

CHINATOWNS

IN THE MID-1800S, MANY CHINESE IMMIGRANTS SETTLED ON THE WEST COAST IN CITIES SUCH AS SAN FRANCISCO AND LOS ANGELES. SOME OF THE IMMIGRANTS TRIED TO STRIKE IT RICH DURING THE CALIFORNIA GOLD RUSH. OTHERS HELPED BUILD THE FIRST RAILROAD TO CROSS THE UNITED STATES.

THESE IMMIGRANTS FORMED COMMUNITIES IN WHICH THEY COULD SHARE THEIR UNIQUE CULTURE AND LANGUAGE. THOSE AREAS ARE CALLED "CHINATOWNS." IN CHINATOWNS, CHINESE IMMIGRANTS BUILT PLACES TO LIVE, SHOP, AND EAT.

THE OLDEST AND LARGEST CHINATOWN IN THE
UNITED STATES IS IN SAN FRANCISCO, WHERE
BRUCE LEE WAS BORN. THE FIRST CHINESE
IMMIGRANTS ARRIVED IN SAN FRANCISCO IN 1848.
THE CHINATOWN AREA IN SAN FRANCISCO IS STILL
A VIBRANT PART OF THE CITY. OTHER US CITIES
THAT HAVE THRIVING CHINATOWNS INCLUDE NEW
YORK AND CHICAGO.

Chapter 2
Back to the States

In 1954, Bruce began studying kung fu under a famous instructor in Hong Kong named Yip Man. (Bruce always wrote "gung fu," which is the way to spell it in the Cantonese dialect in China.)

As a result of this kung fu training, Bruce was learning to protect himself, but he wasn't learning to avoid fights—not yet, anyway. He still got into many fights at school, and after school.

Bruce fought so much that one teacher suggested he enter an inter-school boxing tournament in 1958. Bruce did—and he won!

He easily defeated several opponents by knocking them out in the first round. Then he fought a British student named Gary Elms in the final. Elms had won the tournament three years in a row, but Bruce knocked him out in the third round and won the championship.

Bruce's strength and quickness made him an excellent boxer. His smooth moves and

footwork made him an excellent dancer, too. At about the same time that he won the boxing tournament, he was also a cha-cha dance champion in Hong Kong.

When he was eighteen, Bruce got into a serious fight. The police were called. They knew Bruce and showed up at the door of the Lee family's apartment. "If he gets in one more fight, I'm going to have to put him in jail," one of the policemen warned.

Bruce's parents knew something had to be done. It wasn't an easy choice, but they decided to send him back to the United States. They believed it would keep Bruce out of trouble with the gangs in Hong Kong and that he would get a proper education there.

Lee Hoi Chuen had a friend in Seattle, Washington, who owned a restaurant. He agreed to let Bruce stay in a room above the restaurant and work as a waiter. In April 1959, Bruce

boarded a ship headed for San Francisco.
From there, he made his way to Seattle.
He enrolled at the University of
Washington. A counselor at the
school suggested that he study
philosophy, which is the study
of basic understanding and
wisdom, because of Bruce's
curious nature.

Influenced by his study of philosophy, Bruce began to ask himself lots of questions. He asked, "What comes after victory? Why do people value victory so much? What is glory? What kind of victory is glorious?" What Bruce meant was that he began to question why he had fought so much as a child. What did it reflect about him to the world?

The more Bruce studied philosophy, the more his attitude about fighting started to change. He realized he was wrong to have sought out fights as a youngster. He learned that being prepared was the best way to avoid a fight—not to start one.

While still in college, Bruce began teaching

his friends kung fu. At first, he did it for free. Then some people suggested that he open his own teaching studio. So, while still in college, twenty-two-year-old Bruce opened the Jun Fan Gung Fu Institute in 1963.

From the start, Bruce began including his personal ideas into his kung fu classes. He wasn't only teaching his students to defend themselves, he said. He also was teaching them to express themselves through movement.

One of Bruce's students in Seattle was Linda Emery. Bruce asked her out on a date in October of 1963. They fell in love and soon made plans to get married.

At first, Linda's parents didn't think it was such a good idea. They were worried that Bruce and Linda would move to Hong Kong and live far away. Linda and Bruce, though, were sure they made the right choice. Bruce was a man of "quality, and integrity, and great love, and warmth," Linda said.

"Linda and I aren't one and one," Bruce once said. "We are two halves that make a whole. Two halves fitted together are more efficient than either half would ever be alone!"

On August 17, 1964, less than one year after
their first date, Bruce and Linda were married in

Seattle. In 1965, they had their first child, a son they named Brandon.

The Lee family moved to Oakland. Bruce opened a new studio there. He taught kung fu, but he also began developing his own martial-arts system.

CHA-CHA CHAMP

BRUCE MOVED WITH QUICKNESS, EASE, AND GRACE WHILE PERFORMING KUNG FU. THOSE SAME TRAITS MADE HIM A GREAT DANCER, TOO. IN FACT, HE WAS A CHA-CHA CHAMPION IN HONG KONG BEFORE HE SAILED TO THE UNITED STATES. THE CHA-CHA IS A RHYTHMIC LATIN DANCE THAT STARTED IN 1953. IT QUICKLY BECAME POPULAR IN MUCH OF THE WORLD.

WHEN BRUCE CAME TO THE UNITED STATES BY SHIP IN 1959, HE HAD ONLY ABOUT 100 DOLLARS IN HIS POCKET, AND HE WAS IN ONE OF THE CHEAPER CABINS BELOW DECK. BUT HE SOON MADE EXTRA MONEY FOR THE TRIP BY TEACHING SOME OF THE PASSENGERS IN THE MORE EXPENSIVE CABINS ABOVE TO DO THE CHA-CHA.

Chapter 3
TV Star

A man named Jay Sebring was in the crowd the day in 1964 that Bruce showcased his skills at the First International Karate Tournament in Long Beach, California. Sebring was a friend of

Hollywood producer William Dozier. That's how Dozier came to know about Bruce.

A producer is someone who does lots of the

behind-the-scenes work on a movie or a television program. He or she might do everything from helping to create the show, to hiring the actors and directors, to raising money to make the show. The producer does not appear on camera. But if you've ever seen reruns of the *Batman* television series from the 1960s, you've heard Dozier speak. He's the deep-voiced narrator who says things such as, "Meanwhile, back in the villains' hideout," and, "Tune in next time—same bat-time, same bat-channel!"

Dozier hired Bruce to play the son of a fictional detective named Charlie Chan in a new television series. The series never got off the ground, and eventually the idea was canceled. Dozier liked what he saw of Bruce, however, so when the producer had another chance to hire him for a new television show, he did.

The show was called *The Green Hornet*. It was based on a comic-book character of the same

name, just like *Batman* was. *Batman* was hugely
popular, and Dozier was looking for another hit
show. Dozier wanted Bruce to play the role of the
Green Hornet's sidekick, who was named Kato.
He was the Green Hornet's driver and bodyguard.
The Green Hornet and Kato fought crime
together.

At first, Bruce wasn't sure he wanted to play

that character. Before he came along, Chinese roles in movies and on television were either offensive exaggerations or were played by white actors using silly accents—sometimes both! As Bruce once put it, the dialog for the Chinese characters always included a lot of "ah-sos" and "chop-chops." Bruce didn't want to reinforce those old stereotypes.

"That was his rule," Linda said. "He would not do any roles that were demeaning to the Chinese culture."

Dozier assured Bruce it wouldn't be that way at all. Instead, Kato would use his smarts and martial-arts skills to catch criminals and save the day.

So Bruce took the job, and the Lee family moved to Los Angeles, where *The Green Hornet* was filmed.

The Green Hornet introduced Bruce, who was twenty-five years old at the time, to American TV audiences. His kung fu skills were like nothing ever before seen on television. He moved with amazing speed. One story is that Bruce's reflexes were so fast that he could stand in front of a person who held a coin in an open hand, grab the coin, and replace it with another before the person's hand could close.

Bruce definitely was too fast for the cameras to catch all of his incredible moves. The makers of *The Green Hornet* had to ask him to slow down his action. They didn't think television viewers would believe anyone could move as fast as Bruce without using special effects.

A funny thing happened with the show: Kato turned out to be more popular than the Green

Hornet. That was good for Bruce—but bad for
the show. It lasted only one season. When it was
canceled, Bruce was out of a job.

BATMAN

BATMAN AND *THE GREEN HORNET* WERE TELEVISION SHOWS. THEY WERE EACH ON THE AIR FOR THE FIRST TIME IN 1966. *BATMAN* WAS OUTRAGEOUSLY SILLY AND FUN. IT BECAME WILDLY POPULAR WITH VIEWERS AND WITH HOLLYWOOD STARS WHO WANTED TO PLAY GUEST VILLAINS ON THE SHOW. *THE GREEN HORNET* WAS MORE SERIOUS IN ITS APPROACH, THOUGH. IT NEVER DID AS WELL IN THE RATINGS AS *BATMAN* DID.

THE GREEN HORNET AND KATO APPEARED IN
THREE EPISODES OF *BATMAN*. THE MAKERS OF THE
TWO SHOWS THOUGHT IT MIGHT HELP GENERATE
MORE INTEREST IN *THE GREEN HORNET*.

IN ONE EPISODE, BRUCE LEE'S CHARACTER,
KATO, WAS SUPPOSED TO LOSE A FIGHT TO
BATMAN'S SIDEKICK, ROBIN. BRUCE WOULD HAVE
NONE OF THAT. IN THE END, THE WRITERS
DECIDED ON A TIE.

WHILE *BATMAN* LASTED 120 EPISODES OVER
THREE SEASONS, *THE GREEN HORNET* WAS
CANCELED AFTER ONLY TWENTY-SIX EPISODES
IN ONE SEASON.

After the show was canceled, Bruce and his family decided to stay in Los Angeles. Most movies and television shows were made there, so they figured it would help his acting career to be close by. Soon enough, Bruce landed several parts on television and in the movies.

In 1967 and 1968, Bruce played karate instructors in episodes of the popular crime drama *Ironside* and the comedy *Blondie*. He also guest-starred as a Chinese immigrant in a comedy Western called *Here Come the Brides*. Though he usually played the good guy, he was cast as a bad guy in a movie called *Marlowe* starring James Garner. In the most famous scene in *Marlowe*, Bruce knocks out a light hanging from the ceiling with a kick high above his head!

Still, Bruce's acting career didn't take off quite like he had hoped. He probably wondered if his future would be in teaching the martial arts, after all.

Chapter 4
Martial-Arts Pioneer

When Bruce played Kato on *The Green Hornet*, he introduced millions of television viewers to the martial arts. Because of him, the popularity of kung fu soared in the United States.

Bruce went back to teaching kung fu when the show was cancelled. He had a family to support, after all. He and Linda were busy raising Brandon, who liked to practice kung fu moves just like his dad.

Then, in 1969, Bruce and Linda had their second child, a girl they named Shannon.

When Bruce went back to teaching, stars lined up at his door. Actor James Coburn wanted to learn from Bruce. So did actor Steve McQueen.

One famous director paid
for Bruce to fly to Switzerland
to teach him there! Even seven-
foot two-inch basketball
legend Kareem Abdul-Jabbar
wanted Bruce to teach him.
(Bruce and Abdul-Jabbar
became good friends,
and Bruce eventually
got to cast him as
his opponent in a
movie.)

Bruce
choreographed
the martial-arts
scenes in some
movies. That
means he helped
set up the fights
called for in the

script and showed the actors what to do. One of those movies was called *The Wrecking Crew*. In it, actor Dean Martin plays a spy. Bruce taught Martin how to use kung fu. People in the movie business wanted to learn from the best, and Bruce was the best.

Not everyone was happy about Bruce teaching martial arts. There were two reasons for that.

The first reason was *who* Bruce was teaching. Some people thought it was a bad idea for

Bruce to teach the martial arts to Westerners. (Westerners, or the Western world, is a term to describe cultures, not geography. For example, people from Europe and North America are considered Westerners. People from China, Japan, and the Middle East are considered Easterners, or from the Eastern world.) For hundreds of years, martial arts, such as kung fu, had been taught only by Chinese masters to Chinese students.

Many traditional Chinese people thought it was wrong for Bruce to share kung fu secrets with people who were not Chinese. In fact, when Bruce first started teaching kung fu in Oakland, California, a group of traditional Chinese teachers challenged him to a fight. If their representative beat Bruce, he would have to stop teaching non-Chinese people. Bruce took the challenge and easily won the fight. His studio stayed open, and he continued teaching whomever he wanted.

The second problem some people had with Bruce was over *what* he was teaching. He wasn't sticking to the old ways of teaching martial arts. Bruce didn't believe that any particular martial art was best in all circumstances. After all, he had learned in street fights that opponents are not playing by any rules. You can't defend yourself if you're too worried about how to stand and what technique to use. As he once said, "the proper method is the one that works."

Bruce believed in taking the most useful aspects of the martial arts, simplifying them, and creating his own style. He developed a system called *jeet kune do.* Translated, *jeet kune do* means, "the way of the intercepting fist." But Bruce also liked to call his system "the Way of No Way."

Actually, Bruce never wanted it to be called a "system" at all. He considered *jeet kune do* to be a specific form of training instead of a method of fighting. He didn't like giving it a name. "*Jeet kune do* is merely a name used—a boat to get one across the river," he said. "And once across, it is to be discarded."

Bruce's original training was in kung fu, but he didn't want to be confined by kung fu. He wanted to use all of his talents. "Fighting is not something dictated by your conditioning as a Chinese martial artist or a Japanese martial artist," he said.

To help Westerners understand what he meant, Bruce liked to use the example of a boxer and a wrestler. A boxer likes to have space between him and his opponent so he can extend his arms and deliver strong punches to the other fighter. A wrestler likes to get up close to his opponents so he can grapple with the other fighter.

If a boxer and a wrestler fight each other, neither one of them can rely only on his training to win.

Instead, they need to break free from the form they were taught.

In a street fight, Bruce said, his opponent wouldn't be restricted to any specific method. So why should he? Bruce believed *jeet kune do* freed him from any one method. He boiled down his approach to simple terms: "If the enemy is cool, stay cooler than him. If the enemy moves, move faster than him."

Interestingly, after his teenage years, Bruce hardly ever fought, even in competition. The ancient Chinese general and philosopher Sun Tzu once said, "The supreme art of war is to subdue the enemy without fighting." Bruce echoed those words in one movie, when he described his style as the "art of fighting without fighting." In other words, being an expert in martial arts helped him to avoid fights. Other guys knew Bruce was so good that fighting him would just mean trouble for them.

Of course, that was away from the television and movie screen. On screen, Bruce would eventually become one of the greatest martial-arts fighters of all time.

THE MOST POPULAR MARTIAL ARTS

THERE ARE HUNDREDS OF DIFFERENT MARTIAL-ARTS SYSTEMS OR STYLES WITH ORIGINS ALL AROUND THE WORLD. BRUCE LEE DEVELOPED *JEET KUNE DO* BECAUSE HE BELIEVED ELEMENTS OF VARIOUS MARTIAL ARTS WERE PRACTICAL SOME OF THE TIME, BUT THAT NO MARTIAL ART WAS PRACTICAL ALL OF THE TIME. HERE ARE A FEW OF THE MOST POPULAR AND WELL-KNOWN MARTIAL ARTS:

AIKIDO: A JAPANESE METHOD FOR SELF-DEFENSE. AIKIDO DOES NOT RELY ON PHYSICAL STRENGTH. INSTEAD, IT USES AN ATTACKER'S OWN MOMENTUM TO DEFEAT HIM.

HAPKIDO: ANOTHER MARTIAL ART FOR SELF-DEFENSE, THIS ONE FROM KOREA. IT INCLUDES ELEMENTS OF AIKIDO, BUT ALSO UTILIZES KICKS AND PUNCHES.

JUDO: AN OLYMPIC SPORT SINCE 1964, JUDO EVOLVED FROM THE JAPANESE MARTIAL ART JUJITSU. IN JUDO, THE OBJECT IS TO USE SPEED AND LEVERAGE TO THROW OR TAKE DOWN AN OPPONENT.

JUJITSU: A SYSTEM THAT DEVELOPED AMONG THE SAMURAI WARRIORS OF JAPAN TO DEFEAT ARMED OPPONENTS BY USING HOLDS, THROWS, OR PUNCHES.

KARATE: KARATE EMPHASIZES STRONG, QUICK BLOWS THAT CONCENTRATE POWER AND ENERGY. IT UTILIZES STRIKING TECHNIQUES SUCH AS PUNCHING, KICKING, AND KNIFE HANDS (A "KARATE CHOP"). KARATE ORIGINATED IN WHAT IS NOW PART OF JAPAN.

KUNG FU: A TERM FOR VARIOUS CHINESE MARTIAL ARTS. BRUCE LEE'S EARLIEST MARTIAL-ARTS INSTRUCTION WAS IN A STYLE OF KUNG FU CALLED WING CHUN, WHICH USES STRIKING AND GRAPPLING IN CLOSE FIGHTING.

TAE KWON DO: A KOREAN MARTIAL ART FOR SELF-DEFENSE. IT RELIES MORE HEAVILY ON KICKING THAN MANY OTHER MARTIAL ARTS. TAE KWON DO IS ALSO AN OLYMPIC SPORT.

TAI CHI: AN ANCIENT CHINESE MARTIAL ART. IT IS USED TO IMPROVE PHYSICAL AND MENTAL WELL-BEING THROUGH SLOW, CONTROLLED MOVEMENT.

Chapter 5
Philosopher

Bruce's ability to perform martial arts almost ended in 1970. One morning, he was lifting weights when he felt a pain in his back. The next day, the pain was worse. The day after that, it was worse still. Soon, the pain was unbearable. He went to see a doctor. The doctor told Bruce he had permanently damaged a nerve in his back. He said Bruce's kung fu career was over.

Bruce was confined to bed for the next three months. For three months after that, he still couldn't do any martial arts. That was six full months with no martial-arts training.

"In every big thing or achievement there are always obstacles—big or small," he later said. "The reaction one shows to such obstacles is

what counts, not the obstacle itself."

In this case, Bruce's obstacle was his injury. For the first time in his life, he wasn't in motion. How did he react to it? Well, he didn't mope around feeling sorry for himself. And he didn't waste his time, either. Instead, he continued to develop his philosophy—his personal code of conduct. Bruce read many books on other people's ideas of what the basic principles of life might be. He had a huge library. He once estimated he had more than 2,500 books!

Bruce studied those books, and he thought about a lot of things. He thought about *jeet kune do*. He thought about life. He thought about how he could bring more of his thoughts about life into his teaching of the martial arts.

He also began to write. His notes have been compiled into many different books about *jeet kune do*, the martial arts, and wisdom for everyday living.

Still, Bruce had always been a man on the move, and he needed to get back into action. He knew what the doctor had told him: He set out to prove the doctor wrong.

Bruce mapped out his own strategy for getting better. He started slowly at first, then gradually worked his way back into shape. He had to deal with pain in his back for the rest of his life. Otherwise, though, he was as good as ever.

Bruce was able to return to the martial arts in large part because his ways of training and fitness were revolutionary. His methods were considered extremely unusual for his day, but they have long since become accepted.

Consider weight training, for instance. In Bruce's time, weight training was used mostly by huge bodybuilders who wanted to make their muscles as big as possible. Bruce was only about five-feet seven-inches tall and weighed only 140 pounds. Still, he trained with weights. He didn't

care about how big his muscles were, he cared
how useful they were. Though he was not big, his
strength was legendary. He was so strong that he
could do fifty chin-ups—using only one arm!

THE WISDOM OF BRUCE LEE: A FEW

"I FEAR NOT THE MAN WHO HAS PRACTICED TEN THOUSAND KICKS ONCE, BUT I FEAR THE MAN WHO HAS PRACTICED ONE KICK TEN THOUSAND TIMES."

"NOTICE THAT THE STIFFEST TREE IS MOST EASILY CRACKED, WHILE THE BAMBOO OR WILLOW SURVIVES BY BENDING WITH THE WIND."

OF HIS MOST FAMOUS SAYINGS

"I DON'T BELIEVE IN PURE LUCK. YOU HAVE TO CREATE YOUR OWN LUCK. YOU HAVE TO BE AWARE OF THE OPPORTUNITIES AROUND YOU AND TAKE ADVANTAGE OF THEM."

"IF YOU ALWAYS PUT LIMITS ON EVERYTHING YOU DO, PHYSICAL OR ANYTHING ELSE, IT WILL SPREAD INTO YOUR WORK AND INTO YOUR LIFE. THERE ARE NO LIMITS. THERE ARE ONLY PLATEAUS, AND YOU MUST NOT STAY THERE, YOU MUST GO BEYOND THEM."

"ALWAYS BE YOURSELF; EXPRESS YOURSELF, HAVE FAITH IN YOURSELF, DO NOT GO OUT AND LOOK FOR A SUCCESSFUL PERSONALITY AND DUPLICATE IT."

"THOUGH WE POSSESS A PAIR OF EYES, MOST OF US DO NOT REALLY 'SEE' IN THE TRUE SENSE OF THE WORD."

"IF YOU LOVE LIFE, DON'T WASTE TIME, FOR TIME IS WHAT LIFE IS MADE UP OF."

Bruce also kept strict diet and exercise routines. He took vitamins and Chinese herbs, and his workouts were intense. He even practiced a radical method of electric muscle stimulation. Doctors have since found it to be a valuable tool for helping damaged muscles heal and for preventing

injury to healthy muscles. Bruce was ahead of his time in all these areas.

In 1970, when Bruce had recovered enough from his back injury, he took a trip with Brandon to Hong Kong. That trip would help make him a superstar.

Chapter 6
Cultural Icon

On his trip to Hong Kong in 1970, the twenty-nine-year-old Bruce met adoring fans everywhere he went. When he walked down the street, people ran up to him to say hello. If he ate dinner in a

restaurant, they stared and whispered to their friends. Talk show hosts wanted to interview him. Television variety shows wanted him to give kung fu demonstrations.

Bruce was a little surprised by all the attention. At the time, reruns of *The Green Hornet* were showing on television in Hong Kong. People there didn't call it *The Green Hornet*, though. Instead, Bruce was so popular that they called it *The Kato Show*. They were proud of Kato. Finally, an American television show featured a Chinese character in a strong and positive way.

Bruce's reception in Hong Kong made him think that maybe China was where his film career could really take off. He thought that if he became a big star in Hong Kong then he could move into films in the United States. Plus, there were a lot of good things about making movies in Hong Kong. He could have more influence there on how action films were made. He could make movies the way he wanted which meant that he could help change how the Chinese were perceived in America.

In 1971, Bruce signed a deal with Raymond Chow to do a series of martial-arts action films for a company called Golden Harvest Productions in Hong Kong.

Before Bruce's collaboration with Raymond Chow and Golden Harvest, most Chinese action films were not very good. They used wires to make it look like the actors and martial artists were flying through the air. Bruce knew that those movie tricks only looked silly. He knew that he was better than other Chinese martial-arts actors. He didn't need any special effects.

"Before I made my first Chinese film, Chinese flicks were considered kind of unrealistic," Bruce said. "There was a lot of overacting and a lot of jumping around. All in all, it didn't look real."

Bruce's first movie with Golden Harvest was called *The Big Boss,* released in 1971. (It was titled *Fists of Fury* when it was later released in the United States.)

In *The Big Boss*, Bruce plays a young man named
Cheng. He works in an ice factory with his
cousins. Cheng promises his mom he will never
fight. But when his cousins are killed, he needs

to break that promise and fight the criminals
who are selling drugs out of the factory. *The Big
Boss* marked the first time Bruce had a starring role
in a film.

When *The Big Boss* premiered in Hong Kong, the audience was quiet. Bruce wasn't sure what they thought of it. But after the final scene, when the lights came on in the theater everyone burst into wild applause! They were so quiet during the movie because they were mesmerized. They had never seen anything like it.

Before *The Big Boss*, the movie that made the most money in Asia was *The Sound of Music*, which was an American musical. *The Big Boss* broke *The Sound of Music's* box-office record. But the new record didn't last long. That's because Bruce's second film for Golden Harvest, called *Fist of Fury*, was released in 1972. It broke *The Big Boss's* records. (*Fist of*

Fury was renamed *The Chinese Connection* when it came out in the United States.)

In *Fist of Fury*, Bruce plays a man named Chen Zhen who returns to his old school. Chen Zhen finds out that his favorite teacher, a legendary martial-arts instructor, has been killed. Chen Zhen avenges his teacher's death by fighting a bunch of bad guys.

Fist of Fury, like all Bruce's motion pictures, includes some violent fight scenes. In fact, each of the four movies in which he starred as an adult are rated R ("Children Under 17 Require Accompanying Parent or Adult Guardian"). But Bruce did not want to glorify violence. He said the fighting in his films was action that bordered on fantasy. "I do not believe in playing up violence in films," he said. "I think it is unhealthy."

The Big Boss and *Fist of Fury* were so successful that other companies wanted Bruce to leave Golden Harvest and come work for them. But

Bruce remained loyal to Raymond Chow. And Raymond Chow rewarded that loyalty by giving Bruce control over the next martial-arts action film. Bruce would not only star in *The Way of the Dragon*, which came out late in 1972, but he also would write, produce, and direct the movie.

The script for *The Way of the Dragon* (called *Return of the Dragon* in the United States) was pretty much like the others. Bruce plays Tang Lung, who travels to Rome, Italy, to work with his cousins in a restaurant. When bad guys try to take the restaurant from Tang Lung's cousins, he fights back. The climactic fight is against another great martial artist, Chuck Norris. It takes place in the famous Colosseum in Rome.

The Way of the Dragon was another huge hit. Hollywood was starting to take notice.

BRUCE LEE VS. CHUCK NORRIS

IN THE 2012 MOVIE *THE EXPENDABLES 2*, ONE OF THE CHARACTERS TELLS BOOKER, PLAYED BY CHUCK NORRIS, "I HEARD YOU GOT BIT BY A KING COBRA." TO WHICH BOOKER REPLIES: "YEAH, BUT AFTER FIVE DAYS OF AGONIZING PAIN, THE COBRA DIED."

THAT FAMOUS MOVIE LINE CREDITS NORRIS WITH SUPERHUMAN STRENGTH AND POWER. HE IS NOT SUPERHUMAN. STILL, NORRIS IS A SIX-TIME WORLD PROFESSIONAL MIDDLEWEIGHT KARATE CHAMPION. HE IS A MEMBER OF THE MARTIAL ARTS HISTORY MUSEUM'S HALL OF FAME. IN 1990, HE BECAME THE FIRST WESTERNER IN THE 4,500-YEAR HISTORY OF TAE KWON DO TO EARN THE RANK OF EIGHTH-DEGREE BLACK-BELT GRAND MASTER.

LIKE BRUCE LEE, NORRIS WENT ON TO USE MARTIAL ARTS WHILE STARRING IN ACTION FILMS AND ON TELEVISION. NORRIS, WHO RARELY LOST

IN REAL-LIFE COMPETITIONS, LOST A MOVIE FIGHT ONLY ONCE. THAT WAS AGAINST BRUCE IN *THE WAY OF THE DRAGON.*

THE TWO MARTIAL-ARTS STARS HAD GREAT RESPECT FOR EACH OTHER. SOMETIMES THEY TRAINED TOGETHER. EVEN THOUGH THEY HAD A BIG FIGHT SCENE IN *THE WAY OF THE DRAGON,* THEY WERE ACTUALLY VERY GOOD FRIENDS.

Chapter 7
Gone Too Soon

In the fall of 1972, Bruce was working on another movie in Hong Kong called *Game of Death* (with Kareem Abdul-Jabbar, the basketball star) when he was contacted by Warner Brothers. The big Hollywood studio wanted Bruce, who was then thirty-one years old, to make a motion picture called *Enter the Dragon*. It would be the first time Hollywood and Hong Kong worked together to produce a movie.

Bruce's dream of bringing Chinese culture to Americans was coming true. Bruce believed that people would learn to appreciate the martial arts from his movies, and if they appreciated the martial arts, they also would appreciate Chinese culture. That made Bruce a hero to the Chinese people.

Even though Bruce was living in the United States, his Chinese heritage was still very important to him. He remained close to his family, too. Bruce's father died shortly after Brandon was born in 1965. His mother moved to Los Angeles several years after that to be near Bruce and his family. Bruce's older brothers and sisters were already living in the United States. His younger brother, Robert, was a popular musician in Hong Kong before he, too, moved to Los Angeles.

Bruce knew that *Enter the Dragon* was a great opportunity to "let the outside world in on some of our Chinese culture." He felt an awesome sense of responsibility because of it. If *Enter the Dragon* was going to showcase Chinese traditions and customs, he felt he had to honor them.

Bruce always had worked hard, putting all his boundless energy into his training and films. But now his schedule was incredibly hectic. He

was working around the clock. He was writing
the *Enter the Dragon* script, acting, training, and
choreographing fight scenes.

In May 1973, when working in Hong Kong on the sound for *Enter the Dragon*, Bruce collapsed. He was exhausted. It was a scary incident, but he recovered. Then, on July 20, while working on the script for his next movie, *Game of Death*, Bruce complained of a headache. So he took some medicine and went to sleep.

When it was time for dinner, one of his costars in *Game of Death* couldn't wake him up. Neither could Raymond Chow. They called an ambulance. The ambulance took Bruce to the hospital, and he was declared dead on arrival. He was only thirty-two years old.

The cause of Bruce's death was a cerebral edema, or brain swelling. It was the result of a reaction to the pain medicine. The news was

devastating to Bruce's fans in Hong Kong.
Bruce was so popular that a reported twenty-five
thousand people turned out for his funeral in
Hong Kong. They crammed the city streets as his
funeral procession drove past. They strained police
barricades to get a glimpse of their fallen hero.
Then they respectfully walked by his casket to pay
their final respects.

Bruce's widow, Linda, wanted him buried in
Seattle. That's where she planned to live with
their children, Brandon and Shannon. So another

funeral was held in Seattle, Washington. Actors Steve McQueen and James Coburn helped carry his coffin. Thousands of people still visit Bruce's gravesite in Seattle each year.

BRANDON LEE

BRUCE LED THE WAY FOR OTHER MARTIAL ARTISTS TO STAR IN ACTION FILMS. AMONG THEM ARE CHUCK NORRIS, JEAN-CLAUDE VAN DAMME, STEVEN SEAGAL, CYNTHIA ROTHROCK, AND BRANDON LEE (BRUCE AND LINDA LEE'S SON).

SADLY, BRANDON LEE ALSO DIED AT A YOUNG AGE. IN 1993, HE WAS KILLED BY A FREAK GUNSHOT WOUND WHILE FILMING A MOVIE CALLED *THE CROW*. A GUN THAT WAS SUPPOSED TO FIRE A BLANK CARTRIDGE FIRED A REAL BULLET, AND IT STRUCK BRANDON. HE WAS ONLY TWENTY-EIGHT YEARS OLD.

Chapter 8
The Legend Grows

The line in front of the Chinese Theater
in Hollywood went around the corner. It was

seven-thirty in the evening, and *Enter the Dragon* was scheduled to start in half an hour. But the line wasn't for that show. It was for the ten o'clock show! The 8:00 p.m. screening already was sold out, and people were waiting in line two-and-a-half hours early for the next one.

Enter the Dragon was billed as the "first

American-produced martial-arts spectacular!" It opened in Hollywood on August 24, 1973, just five weeks after Bruce died. Not all the critics loved it, but the public sure did. It seemed like everyone wanted to see it. A movie

that cost less than one million dollars to make went on to take in more than 200 million dollars—making it one of the greatest financial blockbusters of all time.

In *Enter the Dragon*, Bruce plays a Shaolin monk named Lee, who is invited to compete in a martial arts tournament held on the remote island of the mysterious and evil Han. Han is a disgraced former Shaolin student who is now running an empire of crime. He is well protected by the martial-arts talent he has recruited over

the years during his tournaments, and his left
hand is an iron weapon. But he is no match for

Lee, who eventually frees the prisoners on the island and, in one of the movie's most famous

scenes, kills Han with one of his own swords in
a room of mirrored walls.

Bruce had become an
action-movie legend by
the time *Enter the Dragon*
was in theaters. But that
doesn't explain why, four

decades after his death, he is more popular than
ever. There are dozens of websites devoted to him,
and Bruce Lee conventions have been held around
the world. He is so popular that in 2012, the

FISTS OF FURY

San Francisco Giants baseball team held a Bruce
Lee Tribute Night. After all, the city was Lee's
birthplace. Linda Lee threw out the first pitch,
and Shannon Lee sang the national anthem.

Bruce made a lasting impact on the martial arts by bringing kung fu to Westerners and by developing *jeet kune do*. His reach still extends to popular culture. In action films, many martial-arts stars have tried to follow in Bruce's footsteps. In comic books, characters practice *jeet kune do*. In video games, several characters are patterned after Bruce.

In the rapidly growing sport of mixed martial arts (MMA), Bruce's influence is so strong that some people call him the "Father of MMA." That includes Ultimate Fighting Championship (UFC) president Dana White. He talks about the way Bruce believed "you take the good things from every different discipline, use what works, and you throw the rest away."

Shannon Lee, Bruce's daughter, says *jeet kune do* was not the same as MMA, but that it's fair to call Bruce the Father of MMA because he was the first to teach that a complete fighter has to be free of styles.

Athletes, entertainers, and people in all walks of life credit Lee with having a profound influence on their lives.

Bruce brought together the cultures of the United States and China. He taught centuries-old martial-arts techniques to Westerners, and he brought modern moviemaking techniques to Easterners.

"Under the sky, under the heavens, there is but one family," he once said. "It just so happens that people are different."

Bruce is credited with creating an entirely new film genre. He was arguably the greatest martial artist in history. He was a philosopher, a teacher, and an actor. He even wrote poetry. And he did all this while living only thirty-two short years.

"He lived every day as a day of discovery," his wife, Linda, said at his funeral in Seattle. "His thirty-two years were full of living . . . He believed that man struggles to find a life outside himself, not realizing that the life he seeks is within him."

JACKIE CHAN

PERHAPS THE MOST SUCCESSFUL MARTIAL ARTIST ON-SCREEN SINCE BRUCE LEE IS JACKIE CHAN. HE WAS BORN IN HONG KONG IN 1954. WHEN HE WAS SEVENTEEN, HE WORKED AS A STUNTMAN ON *FIST OF FURY*. LATER, HE WORKED ON *ENTER THE DRAGON*, TOO.

AFTER APPEARING IN MANY MOVIES IN HONG KONG, CHAN MOVED TO HOLLYWOOD AND BECAME A BIG STAR IN THE UNITED STATES. HE HAS APPEARED IN MORE THAN 100 MOVIES IN HIS CAREER. MANY OF THEM HAVE BEEN  BIG HITS AT THE BOX OFFICE, INCLUDING THE POPULAR RUSH HOUR SERIES.

CHAN CREDITS BRUCE LEE WITH BEING A BIG INFLUENCE ON HIS CAREER. BUT WHILE MANY MARTIAL-ARTS STARS TRIED TO COPY BRUCE, CHAN BECAME FAMOUS BY DOING THINGS A LITTLE DIFFERENTLY. HE DOES NOT HAVE AS MUCH FORMAL TRAINING IN THE MARTIAL ARTS, AND HE IS KNOWN FOR HIS COMEDY IN HIS MOVIES. "I NEVER WANTED TO BE THE NEXT BRUCE LEE," HE ONCE SAID. "I JUST WANTED TO BE THE FIRST JACKIE CHAN."

TIMELINE OF BRUCE LEE'S LIFE

1940 — Born November 27 in San Francisco, California

1941 — As an infant, makes an uncredited appearance in a movie in Hong Kong called *Golden Gate Girl*

1946 — Has first speaking role in a Cantonese-language film in Hong Kong

1953 — Begins to learn kung fu

1959 — Leaves Hong Kong to live in the United States

1961 — Attends the University of Washington

1964 — On August 2, performs at International Karate Tournament
On August 17, marries Linda Emery

1965 — Bruce and Linda have a son, Brandon Lee, born February 1

1966 — Costars in *The Green Hornet* television series

1967 — Appears in popular *Ironside* television series

1968 — Plays a villain in the motion picture *Marlowe*

1969 — Bruce and Linda have a daughter, Shannon, born April 19

1971 — Stars in *The Big Boss* (renamed *Fists of Fury* in the United States) for Hong Kong's Golden Harvest Studios

1972 — Stars in *Fist of Fury* (renamed *The Chinese Connection* in the United States) for Golden Harvest Studios
Directs, writes, and stars in *The Way of the Dragon*

1973 — Has first major role in a Hollywood film, *Enter the Dragon*
On July 20, dies in Hong Kong at age thirty-two

1993 — Brandon Lee dies in Wilmington, North Carolina, at age twenty-eight

2012 — San Francisco Giants' Bruce Lee Tribute Night

TIMELINE OF THE WORLD

World War II begins	1939
Japan invades Hong Kong and captures it — The United States enters World War II after Japanese planes bomb Pearl Harbor in Hawaii	1941
British and Chinese troops take Hong Kong back from the Japanese — World War II ends	1945
Jackie Robinson of the Brooklyn Dodgers becomes the first black player in the modern era of Major League Baseball	1947
The United States Supreme Court rules that racial segregation in schools is unconstitutional	1954
Disneyland opens in Anaheim, California	1955
Alaska becomes the 49th state in the US — Hawaii becomes the 50th state	1959
John Glenn becomes the first US astronaut to orbit the earth	1962
John F. Kennedy, the president of the United States, is assassinated	1963
The Beatles become a huge hit in the United States	1964
The United States' Neil Armstrong becomes the first man to walk on the moon	1969
US president Richard Nixon makes an historic visit to Communist China	1972
Richard Nixon resigns as president of the United States after the Watergate scandal	1974

BIBLIOGRAPHY

* Koopmans, Andy. **The Importance of Bruce Lee**. San Diego: Lucent, 2002.

Lee, Bruce. **Bruce Lee: The Celebrated Life of the Golden Dragon**. Edited by John Little. Boston: Tuttle, 2000.

Lee, Bruce. **Jeet Kune Do: Bruce Lee's Commentaries on the Martial Way**. Edited by John Little. Boston: Tuttle, 1997.

Lee, Bruce. **Striking Thoughts: Bruce Lee's Wisdom for Daily Living**. Edited by John Little. Boston: Tuttle, 2002.

* Lewis, Jon E. **Bruce Lee**. Philadelphia: Chelsea House, 1998.

Little, John. **The Warrior Within: The Philosophies of Bruce Lee to Better Understand the World Around You and Live a More Rewarding Life**. Chicago: Contemporary Books, 1996.

* Tagliaferro, Linda. **Bruce Lee**. Minneapolis: Lerner Publications, 2000.

Thomas, Bruce. **Bruce Lee: Fighting Spirit**. Berkley, CA: Frog, Ltd., 1994.

* Books for young readers

THE TIME-TRAVELING ADVENTURES OF THE ROBBINS TWINS

THE TREASURE CHEST

"Kids who have outgrown the
'Magic Treehouse' may enjoy this new series."
—*School Library Journal*

Join Felix and Maisie Robbins on their trips through time as they
meet thrilling historical figures as children in *New York Times*
Best-Selling author Ann Hood's *The Treasure Chest*!

www.treasurechestseries.com